COME ON
ALL you
GHOSTS

Books by Matthew Zapruder

Come On All You Ghosts
The Pajamaist
American Linden

COME ON ALL YOU GHOSTS

MATTHEW ZAPRUDER

COPPER CANYON PRESS
PORT TOWNSEND, WASHINGTON

Cover art by Martina Hoffmann

Copper Canyon Press is in residence at Fort Worden State Park in Port Townsend, Washington, under the auspices of Centrum. Centrum is a gathering place for artists and creative thinkers from around the world, students of all ages and backgrounds, and audiences seeking extraordinary cultural enrichment.

LIBRARY OF CONGRESS CATALOGING-IN-PUBLICATION DATA

Zapruder, Matthew, 1967–
  Come on all you ghosts / Matthew Zapruder.
    p. cm.
  ISBN 1–55659–322–8 (alk. paper)
  I. Title.

PS3626.A67C66 2010
811'.6—dc22

                                    2010016787

987654

COPPER CANYON PRESS
Post Office Box 271
Port Townsend, Washington 98368
www.coppercanyonpress.org

Acknowledgments

I would like to thank the editors of the following publications, in which poems in this book (some in different forms) first appeared: *Agriculture Reader, Article, The Awl, Bat City Review, The Believer, Black Clock, Boston Review, Coconut, Columbia Poetry Review, CUNY GC Advocate, Dædalus, Electronic Poetry Review, Forklift Ohio, Fourteen Hills, Free Inquiry, jubilat, The Laurel Review, Lit Mob, Maggy, Mary, The Massachusetts Review, Narrative, The New York Quarterly, notnostrums, Order and Decorum, Painted Bride Quarterly, The Paris Review, Ploughshares, Poetry, Poetry Flash, A Public Space, Puppyflowers, Slate, Tin House, Volt, Zyzzyva.*

"Never to Return" was reprinted in *The Best American Poetry 2009*, edited by David Lehman and David Wagoner. "Sad News" appeared in *Starting Today: 100 Poems for Obama's First 100 Days*, edited by Arielle Greenberg and Rachel Zucker.

Several of the poems in this book first appeared in *For You in Full Bloom*, a limited-edition book from Pilot Books containing reproductions of paintings by Chris Uphues. Special thanks to Chris for his paintings and his titles, as well as to Betsy Wheeler, Meghan Dewar, and Pilot Books. Thanks as well to Cindy Abramson for the use of her title "Automated Regret Machine."

I would also like to thank the following people and institutions, whose support and help were invaluable to me as I wrote these poems: Lannan Foundation; the James Merrill House and Stonington Village Improvement Association; the Poetry Society of America; the American Academy of Arts and Sciences; Christian Lux, Ron Winkler, Martina Hoffmann, and Luxbooks; Primož Čučnik, Ana Pepelnik, and LUD Šerpa; Michael, Joseph, Jess, and everyone at Copper Canyon.

for my father and Sarah

CONTENTS

I

II

III

IV

Come On All You Ghosts

I

Erstwhile Harbinger Auspices

Erstwhile means long time gone.
A harbinger is sent before to help,
and also a sign of things
to come. Like this blue
stapler I bought at Staples.
Did you know in ancient Rome
priests called augurs studied
the future by carefully watching
whether birds were flying
together or alone, making what
honking or beeping noises
in what directions? It was called
the auspices. The air
was thus a huge announcement.
Today it's completely
transparent, a vase. Inside it
flowers flower. Thus
a little death scent. I have
no master but always wonder,
what is making my master sad?
Maybe I do not know him.
This morning I made extra coffee
for the beloved and covered
the cup with a saucer. Skeleton
I thought, and stay
very still, whatever it was
will soon pass by and be gone.

Aglow

Hello everyone, hello you. Here we are under this sky.
Where were you Tuesday? I was at the El Rancho Motel
in Gallup. Someone in one of the nameless rooms
was dying, slowly the ambulance came, just another step
towards the end. An older couple asked me
to capture them with a camera, gladly I rose and did
and then back to my chair. I thought of Paul Celan,
one of those poets everything happened to
strangely as it happens to everyone. In German
he wrote he rose three pain inches above the floor,
I don't understand but I understand. Did writing
in German make him a little part of whoever
set in motion the chain of people talking who pushed
his parents under the blue grasses of the Ukraine?
No. My name is Ukrainian and Ukranians killed everyone
but six people with my name. Do you understand
me now? It hurts to be part of the chain and feel rusty
and also a tiny squeak now part of what makes
everything go. People talk a lot, the more they do
the less I remember in one of my rooms someone
is always dying. It doesn't spoil my time is what
spoils my time. No one can know what they've missed,
least of all my father who was building a beautiful boat
from a catalogue and might still be. Sometimes I feel him
pushing a little bit on my lower back with a palm
made of ghost orchids and literal wind. Today
I'm holding onto holding onto what Neko Case called
that teenage feeling. She means one thing, I mean another,
I mean to say that just like when I was thirteen
it has been a hidden pleasure but mostly an awful pain
talking to you with a voice that pretends to be shy
and actually is, always in search of the question
that might make you ask me one in return.

Schwinn

I hate the phrase "inner life." My attic hurts,
and I'd like to quit the committee
for naming tornadoes. Do you remember
how easy and sad it was to be young
and defined by our bicycles? My first
was yellow, and though it was no Black
Phantom or Sting-Ray but merely a Varsity
I loved the afternoon it was suddenly gone,
chasing its apian flash through the neighborhoods
with my father in vain. Like being a nuclear
family in a television show totally unaffected
by a distant war. Then we returned
to the green living room to watch the No Names
hold our Over the Hill Gang under
the monotinted chromatic defeated Super
Bowl waters. 1973, year of the Black Fly
caught in my Jell-O. Year of the Suffrage Building
on K Street NW where a few minor law firms
mingle proudly with the Union of Butchers
and Meat Cutters. A black hand
already visits my father in sleep, moving
up his spine to touch his amygdala. I will
never know a single thing anyone feels,
just how they say it, which is why I am standing
here exactly, covered in shame and lightning,
doing what I'm supposed to do.

Automated Regret Machine

My friend and I were watching television
and laughing. Then we saw
white letters begin to crawl along
the bottom of the screen.
People were floating on doors and holding
large pieces of cardboard
with telephone numbers scrawled
in black fear up to the helicopters.
The storm had very suddenly
come and now it was gone.
I saw one aluminum rooftop flash
in sunlight, it would have burned
the feet of anyone trying to wait there.
My friend by then had managed
to will her face into that familiar living
detachment mask. I thought
of the very large yellow house
of the second half of my childhood, how through
my bedroom window I could reach my hand
out and upward and touch
the branch of an elm. At night
in the summer I heard the rasp
of a few errant cicadas whose timing
devices had for them tragically drifted.
And the hoarse glassy call
of the black American crow.
Though I am at least halfway through
my life, part of my spirit
still lives there, thinking very soon
I will go down to the room where my father
carefully places his fingers on the strings of the guitar
he bought a few years before I was born.

Picking his head up he smiles
and motions vaguely with his hand, communicating
many contradictory things.

Poem (for Grace Paley)

People say they don't understand poetry.
Meaning how must we proceed. Be extremely
tempered. Dream a careful dream. People
say we're living a quiet life, lost in a forest
of pronouns, asleep for a thousand years.
People said his wife passed through him
an arrow made of smoke. People say whatever
you do don't hitch a ride on a sepulcher.
People said it was the future then, and we
liked falling into mirrors. People said
we were never sorry we couldn't travel both
and be one traveler. People said what
was it like. It was like an airport terminal
without any televisions. Like waiting
a long time for a door to arrive. In *Outlaw
Josey Wales* Chief Dan George says that
rock candy's not for eating it's for looking
through. In 1981 an announcer said Ralph
Sampson's so tall he could reach out
and touch Uranus. I was thirteen, Earth
was a couch, without any irritable reaching
after fact or reason I placed thousands of
Sweet Tarts into my mouth. Five years
later someone said they saw Diane P.
kissing a girl in a car, and they punched
the window on the passenger side
in and I laughed, and it's all been as
people say downhill from there, meaning
until this moment I have been coasting,
but from this one forward Grace I vow
I shall coast no more.

Pocket

I like the word pocket. It sounds a little safely
dangerous. Like knowing you once
bought a headlamp in case the lights go out
in a catastrophe. You will put it on your head
and your hands will still be free. Or
standing in a forest and staring at a picture
in a plant book while eating scary looking wildflowers.
Saying pocket makes me feel potentially
but not yet busy. I am getting ready to have
important thoughts. I am thinking about my pocket.
Which has its own particular geology.
Maybe you know what I mean. I mean
I basically know what's in there and can even
list the items but also there are other bits
and pieces made of stuff that might not
even have a name. Only a scientist could figure
it out. And why would a scientist do that?
He or she should be curing brain diseases
or making sure that asteroid doesn't hit us.
Look out scientists! Today the unemployment rate
is 9.4%. I have no idea what that means. I tried
to think about it harder for a while. Then
tried standing in an actual stance of mystery
and not knowing towards the world.
Which is my job. As is staring at the back yard
and for one second believing I am actually
rising away from myself. Which is maybe
what I have in common right now with you.
And now I am placing my hand on this
very dusty table. And brushing away
the dust. And now I am looking away

and thinking for the last time about my pocket.
But this time I am thinking about its darkness.
Like the bottom of the sea. But without
the blind fluorescent creatures floating
in a circle around the black box which along
with tremendous thunder and huge shards
of metal from the airplane sank down and settled
here where it rests, cheerfully beeping.

After Reading Tu Fu, I Emerge from a Cloud of Falseness

wearing a suit of light.

It's too easy to be

strange. I glow

reading a few pages

of an ancient Chinese poet

to calm me, but soon

I am traveling down

terrible roads

like an insect chased

by golden armies.

Then I am tired in a little boat

filling with smoke.

Then in the seasonably

cold morning I am

once again missing my friends.

Some have been sent

to the capital to take

their exams or work for a while

or be slowly executed. I

cannot help them, I am trying

to build a straw hut

beside the transparent river.

The sky is a perfect

black dome, with stars

that look white but

are actually slightly blue.

I have two precious candles

to last me a night

that has suddenly come.

I feel the lives of cities

drift through me,

I am a beautiful scroll

on which the history

of a dynasty has been written

in a dead language

not even one lonely scholar knows.

I see sad crushed plastic

everywhere and put

some thoughts composed

of words that do not

belong together

together and feel

a little digital hope.

The Prelude

Oh this Diet Coke is really good,
though come to think of it it tastes
like nothing plus the idea of chocolate,
or an acquaintance of chocolate
speaking fondly of certain times
it and chocolate had spoken of nothing,
or nothing remembering a field
in which it once ate the most wondrous
sandwich of ham and rustic chambered cheese
yet still wished for a piece of chocolate
before the lone walk back through
the corn then the darkening forest
to the disappointing village and its super
creepy bed and breakfast. With secret despair
I returned to the city. Something
seemed to be waiting for me.
Maybe the "chosen guide" Wordsworth
wrote he would even were it "nothing
better than a wandering cloud"
have followed which of course to me
and everyone sounds amazing.
All I follow is my own desire,
sometimes to feel, sometimes to be
at least a little more than intermittently
at ease with being loved. I am never
at ease. Not with hours I can read or walk
and look at the brightly colored
houses filled with lives, not with night
when I lie on my back and listen,
not with the hallway, definitely
not with baseball, definitely
not with time. Poor Coleridge, son

of a Vicar and a lake, he could not feel
the energy. No present joy, no cheerful
confidence, just love of friends and the wind
taking his arrow away. Come to the edge
the edge beckoned softly. Take
this cup full of darkness and stay as long
as you want and maybe a little longer.

Burma

[handwritten: THE ABSOLUTE GRAVITY OF THE FIRST LINE]

In Burma right now people are screaming.
Inside their monasteries the monks are sealed.

"Blood and broken glass."
I feel I would drink a glass of poison,

In order to help,
But that's probably a lie. *[handwritten: HONESTY —]*

Another perfect day filled with perfectly vertical light and crickets.
I feel the presence of lithium. *[handwritten: A LIE]*

They are pumping it into our waters.
I want to do important work.

People not places are haunted.
Who is in that chair?

I want to stop pretending.
I don't feel like I'm pretending, *[handwritten: O'HARA]*

But I want to be free
Of this important feeling:

To love each·other more
Than we currently do

Is a terrible violence
To our future selves.

Which is not what I want.

As I Cross the Heliopause at Midnight, I Think of My Mission

Drunker than Voyager 1
but not as Voyager 2 I rode my blue
bike back through the darkness
to my lonely geode cave of light
awaiting nothing under the punctured
dome. I had achieved escape
velocity drinking clear liquid starlight
at the Thunderbird with a fingerless
Russian hedge fund inspector and one
who called himself The Champ. All
night I felt fine crystals cutting
my lips like rising up through
a hailstorm. And the great vacuum
cleaner that cannot be filled moved
through my chest, gathering
conversation dust and discharging
it through my borehole. During
one of many silences The Champ
took off his face and thus were many
gears to much metallic laughter
revealed. Long ago I forgot
the word which used to mean in truth
but now expresses disbelief. So
quickly did my future come. You who
are floating past me on your inward way,
please inform those glowing faces
who first gave me this shove I have
managed to rotate my brilliant
golden array despite their instructions.

Lamp Day

All day I've felt today is a holiday,
but the calendar is blank.
Maybe it's Lamp Day. There is
one very small one I love
so much I have taken it everywhere,
even with its loose switch.
On its porcelain shade are painted
tiny red flowers, clearly
by someone whose careful
hand we will never know.
Because it's Lamp Day I'm trying
to remember where I got it,
maybe it was waiting for me
in the house on Summer Street
I moved into almost exactly
17 years ago. I think
without thinking I just picked it
up from the floor and put it
on my desk and plugged
it into the socket and already
I was working. So much
since that moment has happened.
On Lamp Day we try
not dreamily but systematically
to remember it all. I do it
by thinking about the hidden
reasons I love something
small. When you take
a series of careful steps
to solve a complex problem,
mathematicians call it an algorithm.
It's like moving through

a series of rooms, each with
two doors, you must choose one,
you can't go back. I begin
by sitting on a bench in the sun
on September 21st thinking
all the walks I have taken
in all the cities I have chosen
to live in or visit with loved ones
and alone make a sunlit
and rainy map no one
will ever be able to hold.
Is this important? Yes and no.
Now I am staring
at clean metal girders.
People keep walking past
a hotel, its bright
glass calmly reflecting
everything bad and good.
Blue boots. Bright glass.
Guests in this moment. A child
through the puddles steps
exuberant, clearly feeling the power.
I am plugged in. I am calm.
Lamp Day has a name.
Just like this cup
that has somehow drifted
into my life, and towards which
sometimes for its own reasons
my hand drifts in turn.
Upon it is written the single
word Omaha.

Poem for Hannah

The tiny bee on its mission
died before it felt a thing. Its
body rested for a moment
on the railing of my sunny
porch in California. Then
wind took it away. You
are an older sister now so
it's true the world owes you
massive reparations. Also
you have special alarm
pheromones implanted
in your nose that explode
with *Phacelia distans*
i.e. wild heliotrope each time
what they say will happen
turns out to be a compendium
of what can never exactly
be. Today the electric bus
full of humans listening
through tiny flesh colored
earbuds to the music news
or literature perfectly calibrated
to their needs kneels before
the young man in his gleaming
black wheelchair. Inside
green laboratories experiments
in the realm of tiny particles
are being for our vast benefit
completed. Already I can see
the same little wrinkle I have
appearing on your brow.
You were born to feel a way
you don't have a word for.

Dobby's Sweatshirt

With those two words in my mouth
I woke up laughing, for only the second
time in my life. Before bed I had been
reading a book about the Renaissance.
All they really know is it was dirty.
I slept and dreamt of complicated
financial arrangements. Then
the Midwest. I have always loved
the loneliness of those midsized cities
strewn along the plains, in them
it seems to me my heart would at last
be that open field where an entirely
new love could snow. Dobby lives
in Minnesota and seems basically happy.
I believe I've never seen him
wear a sweatshirt. I'm not even sure
that's his real name. Is he a ghost?
Probably. A ghost of happiness. Dobby's
sweatshirt. It's where I want to bury
my face when lonely possibility comes.

The New Lustration

Last night I heard faint music moving
up through the floor. The thought
I could be one who falls asleep and dreams
some brave act and wakes to actually
do it flapped through me, brief breeze
through a somnolent flag. Across
the room my cell phone periodically
shone a red light indicating someone
was failing to reach me. Your body
kept barely lifting the sheet. I think
my late night thoughts and feelings
about my life are composed
of fine particles that drift far from me
to periodically settle on apartment
or office buildings. Feel the heat
and pulsation within. A man sits
in the Institute of National Memory
examining files. They contain accounts
of what certain people believed other
more powerful people would want
to permit themselves to believe
regular people were choosing to do
all through the years that like terrible
ordinary babies one after another
crawled, grasping daily acts and placing
them into these files anyone now
can hold. Read about the life
of the great ordinary Citizen Z. How
he attended funerals and horrible boring
literary parties, aging and thinking
of his anonymity and writing journals
he later felt he must destroy, and calmly

against his will periodically meeting
in hotel bars with the sad men who asked
questions that along with the answers
they all knew would end in these yellow files.
Each has a label marked with three
or four obscure numbers followed by
a dash followed by three initials.
Europe you had your time. Now
it is ours to drag everyone into a totally
ghost free 21st century whiteness.

Never to Return

Today a ladybug flew through my window. I was reading
about the snowy plumage of the Willow Ptarmigan
and the song of the Nashville Warbler. I was reading
the history of weather, how they agreed at last
to disagree on cloud categories. I was reading a chronicle
of the boredom that called itself The Great Loneliness
and caused a war. I was reading mosquitoes rode
to Hawaii on the same ship that brought the eucalyptus
to California to function now as a terrible fire accelerator.
Next to me almost aloud a book said doctors can
already transplant faces. Another said you know January
can never be June so why don't you sleep little candle?
A third one murmured some days are too good,
they had to have been invented in a lab. I was paging
through a book of unsent postcards. Some blazed
with light, others were a little dim as if someone
had breathed on the lens. In one it forever snowed
on a city known as the Emerald in Embers, the sun had
always just gone behind the mountains, never to return,
and glass buildings over the harbor stayed filled with
a sad green unrelated light. The postcard was called
The Window Washers. In handwriting it said
Someone left an important window open, and Night
the black wasp flew in and lay on the sill and died.
Sometimes I stop reading and find long black hairs
on my keyboard and would like you to know that in 1992
I mixed Clairol Dye #2 with my damaged bleached hair
to create a blue green never seen before, my best look
according to the girl at the counter who smiled only once,
I know less than I did before, and I live on a hill where
the wind steals music from everything and brings it to me.

II

Together Yet Also Apart || *WHAT AN AWFUL TITLE*

Go we must in search of searching || *CRAZY SYNTAX*
not very helpfully said the little red ant
attached to the golden chain attached to
my wrist. He was no bigger than a
molecule, the chain was a quantum chain.
It was Sunday morning, we were
following the restless backpackers into
the city guidebooks called a manageable
fountain of leisure. Unbeknownst they
carried dark lanterns, they were
Nameless ones. The inhabitants into
various churches emptied leaving only
scattered women in multicolored house
coats feeding pigeons and a boy skater
performing slenderly his fabulous tricks.
Some parks are small, perfect for falling
asleep. Then you can wake and leave
them for someone who needs to find
out what happens when you build
a grand arcade of your finest thoughts
to shimmer, waiting for no one. I lay on
my back. Light with the faintest tetrophene
hint touched lightly my blue metallic skin.
A bike leaned against a wall. I thought
of my first day planner, turquoise and
laminated not unlike the calm and glassy
lake I broke the surface of as a child
those days everyone was equal. So much
architecture, said my russet friend. He
was a menshevik, red but also transparent.
If you bent and looked very closely
you could see the pulse behind each of

his black ventricular eyes. A golem
stopped to check his touristical map.
He wanted to see a few more rooftops
against the sky before he sighed and
took the funicular up the long curved
path that leads to the castle and turned
totally unlike me into dust.

They

I remember the house
where I first lived, it was
small and wooden
and next door to a loud
friendly catholic family
whose three sons Andy
and something and something
else constantly with mysterious
lack of effort flicked
an orange basketball
through a rusty hoop
and one afternoon taught
me *duh*. Once
a car screeched and hit
a girl whose name
I just remembered Julia!
We weren't there
but came running out,
it was quiet and we stood
a little away from the man
from the car who stood
over her, there was
a dark spot on her leg,
it was broken, she was fine.
But they decided to limit
the danger by making
the street one way
with a speed limit of 30.
Who were they?
Since then they have been
here looking over
my shoulder, sometimes

taking care, at others
making the wrong decisions
leading to more bad things.
There's no way
to talk about it
except maybe right now.
Now when I look
at photographs of me
and the twins I hear
the green glass beads
separating my bedroom
from theirs clicking in my mind,
is that a memory? Or
what I know those
sorts of beads sound like
in a breeze? Every day
one block up to Connecticut Ave.
and over to Oyster
Bilingual where I sometimes
was asked to stand
in front of the class and hold
up the picture of a duck
or a house when the teacher
said the words in Spanish
and English both. I played
Santa in the Christmas play
which made sense.
One day Luis stabbed
another kid with a pencil
in the throat, he was also fine.
Another day I went to visit
a friendly girl and ran
straight through the plate glass
window in her apartment building
lobby and out the door

and home, my parents
never knew, I was as I would
now say unscathed. Soon
after we moved to Maryland
where the new Catholics
were threatened and mean,
but that's a different story
I don't yet remember.
I think once a parent dies
the absence in the mind
where new impressions would
have gone is clear, a kind
of space or vacuum related memories
pour into, which is good.

Looking Up

from a book I was reading about
a dead architect I saw not the fabulous
empty pale blue almost white desert
sky above the brand new sewage
treatment plant. Nor my handwriting
in which I had thankfully never written
with a huge glowing made of fire
finger stellar advertisements for starlight
in the sky. Just a few artificial contrails
made by jets on their way to Denver
for me with my eyes to follow,
fading like the thought that had made
me raise my face to catch them
at all. Now only the pure white drug
interdiction blimp tethered to a bristling
radar installation remains, scanning
the sixty or so miles between here
and the border for movement dispositive
of a human trying to survive. Goodbye
Robert Creeley, you died looking out
over the plains. No more will
your fractured days emerge for us
to live a little while in, though we have
your collected poems of which
there are many. And farewell Kenneth
Koch, whom I also never met.
Reading his kaleidoscopes causes me
to wonder if perhaps he is not
a lawn chair, knocked over last night
by a pack of javelina that scared
Richard awake and made him wander
to his table, still half asleep. Or

a blue telephone, waiting in the forest
to ring. This book you are holding
is about dying, as will be the next one
upon which you lay your hands.
Thank you for listening. Now let us
all go separately into the city and forget
everything but our little prescriptions.

April Snow

Today in El Paso all the planes are asleep on the runway. The world
is in a delay. All the political consultants drinking whiskey keep
their heads down, lifting them only to look at the beautiful scarred
waitress who wears typewriter keys as a necklace. They jingle
when she brings them drinks. Outside the giant plate glass windows
the planes are completely covered in snow, it piles up on the wings.
I feel like a mountain of cell phone chargers. Each of the various
faiths of our various fathers keeps us only partly protected. I don't
want to talk on the phone to an angel. At night before I go to sleep
I am already dreaming. Of coffee, of ancient generals, of the faces
of statues each of which has the eternal expression of one of my feelings.
I examine my feelings without feeling anything. I ride my blue bike
on the edge of the desert. I am president of this glass of water.

Little Voice

I woke this morning to the sound of a little voice
saying this life, it was good while it lasted, but I just
can't take it any longer. I'm going to stop shaving
my teeth and chew my face. I'm going to finish inventing
that way to turn my blood into thread and knit
a sweater the shape of a giant machete and chop
my head right off. The leaves had a green
aspect, all their faces turned down towards the earth.
This is exactly how I wanted to act, but I didn't
know where the little voice had hidden, and anyway
who talks like that? What a loss, another tiny
brilliant mind switched off by that same big boring finger.
Clearly life is a drag, by which I mean a net that keeps
pulling the most unsavory and useful boots we
either put on lamenting, or eat with the hooks of some
big idea gripping the sides of our mouths and yanking them
upward in a conceptual grimace. Said the little voice,
that is. I was just half listening, one quarter wondering
what the little park the window looked onto was named,
and one quarter thanking the war I knew was somewhere
busy returning all those limbs to their phantoms.

TONE —
HOW DOES
THIS
WORK?

Never Before

My neighbors, my remnants, in what have you chosen
to bury your heads? Shadow, said one mote
in an auditorium after a lecture. Some
archive explorer had just finished discussing
a group of islands. Inside me for a while
a tribe had theorized purely and wrongly
its location merely on the basis of tides. I was
feeling extinct, and wishing for a sudden
totally silent sliding out from the wall of twenty
or so very excellent beds so we the audience
could together engage in further collective
dreaming. I would describe that lecturer's voice
as twilight shadow smeared origami cloudlet
but the historical ceiling gilded by the names
of agreed-upon great thinkers is a beautiful dowager
making her sleepy wishes into dimness
soon to retire gracefully known. I hear soft
seventies cell phone songs. Come home
those who love a librarian aspect. I am one,
for give her time and she will answer any question
no matter how spiral, no matter how glass,
so slow to judgment you can sit among her
like a reading room and read and think
until the docents come, they move as trained,
as trained they place a careful hand on our shoulder.
The door locks automatically but not before
wind slips in to do its research on blackness
which gets even blacker, on the fabulous black
dust intercom orchard of what happens
when people fall asleep in their dreams and dream
what they are. Have I mentioned lately
I have been reading a book about a steam powered

carriage we are actually in moving slowly
through the countryside towards the kingdom
and its ruined citizens? Have I mentioned tonight
we shall both stand before the enormous spiral
of wrecking balls in a dress made of laughing glass?

Yellowtail

The wind made a little movement
as if it were trying to reassemble.
I looked up from my affidavit. Sometimes
my life feels taped, and quiet evenings
I listen back. I hear the humming of the car
and through the windshield see the road
twisting down a series of cliffs to a very small
blue ocean that like the placid eye
of a beast that regarded our lives without
any desire to eat them grew larger
and stared a little past us, absently
flecked with gold. I would like now to believe
I felt like a leaf. Each night I told
my brother and sister ever more fabulous
stories about far away humanoid beings
with ordinary loves and concerns
swept up into galactic battles for peace
in which the dark forces
with their superior weapons and numbers
were always defeated by a ragtag company
led by slightly better versions of us. No one
ever asked where we were going.
It was all very clear without anyone
saying the dunes and the sea
would never hurt us. Every morning
I opened my eyes so gently I hardly
noticed the difference. Before I was even
awake I would already be flying
a Japanese kite, or sitting underneath
my favorite tree, biting my nails. Perhaps
I am still not supposed to say
advanced translucent beings with the spirits

of animals walked among us. Light
brushed their human hair and cast
their shadows across the tree trunks
or our faces among our games. Someone
was always strumming a guitar with a bird
made of pearl inlaid at the edge of the sound hole
and singing a tune about how helpful
most people are, especially strangers.

You Have Astounding Cosmic News

Dear sociologists, I have been asked to explain poetry to you. Thus
in the offices of dazed lute press the clicking begins. Lately
we've been conducting field experiments into our private thoughts. One
faction next to the soul shaped watercooler wonders whether
there's any reason at all to remember the feeling of being a child. Is
it best to imagine oneself again beneath the desk as the rusted
air raid siren explodes with its bi-monthly ritual Wednesday afternoon
fear distribution? Like you I was always holding particular crayons
in the dimness of certain morning assemblies. I have been told
some of you think the only constant is constant observation. I know
city planners designed the city and still there are diffusionists who pace
the deep blue edge of do you know you can never try to discover
why why flowers in the cubicles. Between you and me the buildings
also have a space for the sparrow named never who does not sing
yes the cities die when you leave them, yes no one cares what you do.
The glass covered in dust windows of the thrift store display
a mirror from the 1920s. If you take it it will no longer regard young
lovers with important thoughts pushed towards the mighty river. I
will fall in love exactly about a million times and then I will die. Clouds
playing dominos agree. At Everest on Grand someone eats yak discussing
the endless undeclared war among the neutral provinces. Long
metallic articulated girders cast thin shadows over thousands of windows.
A photograph of a pacifist smiles. He wore a white suit, was a friend
to the poor and worked for the union of unemployed telegraph workers
who listen for signals pulsing as Joni Mitchell never said from the heart of
a distant star. He was like my grandfather, after he died the city fathers
did not know what they were building when they built a museum
to encase a window in a wall brought from a far away country where
it once overlooked the sea. Evenings through giant speakers people listen
to troubled sounds whales bounce off continental shelves. Go tell
everyone everything is related, the rich own the clouds, and you can
always locate yourself with so many shadows to instruct you.

Poem for Tony

Sometime around 11 p.m. the you I was thinking of
left my head. I was in bed, among my white ten billion
thread count cotton sheets. The pillowcases cradled
my head like the earth a very young carrot.
This very white moment of being alone without
any loneliness I ruled and was ruled by like a benevolent
dictator full of human feelings he manages each day
to actualize for the benefit of his people. He feels
very protective about their souls. To him they seem
to be either tiny milagros in the form of boots
or horses made of pounded flat silver, like the pieces
in the homemade board game that glowed
the way they did just a little when it was his turn
as a child to choose which would represent him,
or small blue aspersions cast like the outside
part of an innocent candle flame that does not burn
your finger if you move it very quickly across.
This moment will never return. You were gone,
for a while I heard crickets and some kind of bird
doing something there is probably a word for between
hooting and whistling. Then the train, which despite
all those songs is not very mysterious at all.

Poem for John McCain

Today I read about the factory
where they make the custom rolling ladders

everyone has probably seen
rising through silent rooms

full of boxes or shelves

crossed by motes in the sun

#5 is my favorite
made of black walnut
with its hinge that folds a small surface out

for reading or placing
books on as you shelve them

it's easy to imagine working in a library

for me at least there is something shameful
about how clearly I can see it

like I am thinking something important is not

I say tomorrow waits for me
but I don't know

if I knew anything about the wars
besides what I have been safely told

I might understand
why they call him a maverick

when he is really just a horse

a horse like me except with dark eyes
terrible from his useless suffering

When It's Sunny They Push the Button

and the sky

through the oval aperture

above your head in the form

of light that bounces

a little then rests on the walls

and also in the form of whatever colors

you can see and maybe

if you're lucky clouds

pours through

maybe it's obvious

and peacefully alien like a young nun

walking past the local establishments

in a university town in summer

where it's always despite the superficial changes

the same time

even the rain

feels like rain after the evacuation

and even happiness

feels like having survived something

I can't remember

Work

This morning I rode my gray metal bike
through the city throwing its trucks at me,
sometimes along the narrow designated
lanes with white painted symbolic bicyclists
so close to the cars too close to my shoulders,
and sometimes down alleys where people
on piles of clothes lie sleeping or smoking
or talking in the shade. Cars parked there
have signs in their windows that the doors
are unlocked and there is no radio.
It is remarkable to me that downtown
is always so remarkable to me. Every single
time I feel so shiny mixing my intention
with all the other lives, each so much
more interesting and easy for me to imagine
than the tourists muttering to each other
over their maps in some garbled
by traffic or wind foreign language I never
quite hear. From my window the old
brick factory building with its large white
graceful letters seems to be actually
proudly saying WILLIAM HENRY STEEL
to the sky, the building floats, up and to
the right but it's the clouds of course
that move. Or is it? The earth moves,
farther off a squat little tower with three
huge metal cylinders that must be
for sending some invisible electric
particles out into the city. I only feel
free when I am working, that is writing
this book about a pair of zombie detectives
who painstakingly follow clues they think

are hidden in an authentic tuscan cookbook.
It is really more a sort of transcribing,
every day I close my eyes and see
them in an ancient yet modern high ceilinged
earth-toned kitchen, laughing as they
blunder through the recipes, each day
a little closer towards the name of their killer
whose face will soon to all of us be clear.
They have a little zombie dog, I name him
William Henry Steel, and this will be
my great work time has brought me here to do.

Lesser Heights Are Bathed in Blue

I'm staring out the window at an aluminum shed.
Periodically late March sun against its roof
flashes just randomly enough not to be a message.
A dog has wandered into the yard. He
keeps crouching until his balls I presume
touch the ice and he jumps and yelps.
What I find hilarious shames me. I am
house sitting. I am sitting in the house
watching ESPN. Daisuke pronounced
Dice K Matsuzaka throws a gyroball, very
slowly it seems to but does not spin
like a green dress on a mannequin in the sun.
I grow hungry awaiting instructions.
On television the cherry blossom festival
has begun. Already the trees have started
to bloom, along the edges their white
leaves turn a slightly deathly darker red.
Every spring amid the day we light
a giant paper lantern the Japanese presented
to us in 1951. Here I am hanging
a black light bulb in an enormous desert for you.
From what? People, I grew up a wonderful
sullen boy close enough to the capitol
building to dream of hitting it with a stick,
but did not. Inside there's an arch
the exact color of the sky, under it anyone
can stand and barely speak and all the way
across the rotunda someone else can hear.
Now it is known as the Millard Fillmore
spot, but only to me. The world's last
remaining Whig, I lie on my back thinking
we must defeat them, but later, after

this final highlight. A giant foam finger
the color of a fabulous foreign lime appears.
I put it on. Wildly I am cheering for nothing. So much
for someone who doesn't remember his dreams.

Minnesota

This blue vinyl couch
you bought is winter sky color,
blue but also a little white
with cracks like the robin's egg
that fell onto the balcony.
The railing is painted
that green generally intended
by the authorities to make you feel
you are not even intentionally
being punished. For weeks
I did nothing but dream
I was writing a letter
to my younger self full
of useless benevolent warnings.
I wasn't lonely, I was 22
and knew lots of things
I've now forgotten like how
they made the great rivers in Siberia
run backward, there's a city
called Ólafsfjörður where every
winter hulls are left locked
in ice so they do not rust,
and what all of that had
to do with me. Now on my back
in Minnesota I am reading
about phlox. The blue
phlox is blue and can grow
to such great heights it will
no longer fit in any more poems.
Unlike in the Young Drift Plains
or southern tip of the Canadian Shield
glaciers here did not as they

melted deposit fertile soil,
only boulders and stones. I see
a squirrel I recognize. It's so
silent I can hear his onyx nails
click on the frozen snow.
He watches a tree until it moves.
He has one main and an alternate nest,
and lives with other squirrels
in a temporary winter community
called an aggregation. I hope
no great watchman comes
with claws to take him
in the night before he can master
techniques of gliding
from tree to tree, so he can
find just what he needs, for that
is what he is looking for.

Starry Wizards

Under the dark blue pre-night sky I stood
holding a flag I had cut from an obsolete windbreaker
and painted with the green fluorescent initials
of our brand new organization. Because of some
quality of the disintegrated light everyone
was a silhouette. William teetered on stilts beneath
the unmistakable hat of Abraham Lincoln. Lula
was the adorable giant robotic rabbit that marched
through our favorite television program harmlessly
ruining the plans of the space fleet authorities
as they endlessly circled our atmosphere in the not
too distant future, waiting for enemy beings
or rogue asteroids that never came. We were
a ragtag collection of young collectors.
We felt enthusiasm for the tentative friendships
we had after long years of hiding from each other
on the breezeway at last and almost too late
aggregated to protect our enthusiasms. Someone's
pet cat was lazily stalking someone else's
giant pet snail. It was all too good to be true
or last. Soon we would all be graduating and along
would amble the appropriate goons to gather
us into the welcoming arms of our new apprenticeships.
We knew if we went wherever we wanted
the starry wizards would guide us, and
if we didn't we would never see them again.

Paper Toys of the World

Friends, what is beauty? Right now for me these paper replicas
I glanced at in a book I did not buy. *Paper Toys of the World.* I hardly
think of anyone but myself. For a little while right now
I know many tiny pagodas were built with knowledge they are not
meant to last. There was paper and there was time someone
had to consider, time no one was in crisis, time no one was dying.
I think each breath the maker sent through them is like
a trusting class of architects sent through an ancient building
where used to be copied terrifying decrees. I bet people
who build pagodas are people who think they won't ever see them.
That thought is true, people know people and I am one. I like
saying this morning in Houston contains many tiny pagodas of wishing
for better things for people we do not know. I like knowing
somewhere social workers consider their clients. Last night Tonya said
I worry too much, she said it softly and firmly because she hardly knows me
and knew I worry I worry she's wrong. Here she is in my thoughts
along with all this beautiful silver fear, beautiful because
it with a silver penumbra protects the family readying itself
for school and work. So I choose to believe and choose to ask you
to believe it too. Today we are driving through the Painted Desert
where a few people live and breathe, it seems possible, Vic says look out
the window and feel and that's what I'm going to do.

Poem

Your eyes are not always brown. In
the wild of our backyard they are light
green like a sunny day reflected
in the eyes of a frog looking
at another frog. I love your love,
it feels dispensed from a metal tap
attached to a big vat gleaming
in a giant room full of shiny whispers.
I also love tasting you after a difficult
day doing nothing assiduously.
Diamond factory, sentient mischievous
metal fruit hanging from the trees
in a museum people wander into thinking
for once I am not shopping. I admire
and fear you, to me you are an abyss
I cross towards you. Just look
directly into my face you said and I felt
everything stop trying to fit. And
the marching band took a deep collective
breath and plunged back into its song.

Poem for Ferlinghetti

Everything I know about birds
is I can't remember plus
two of the four mourning
also known as rain
doves, the young ones
born in my back yard
just this April. I saw
them moving their wings
very rapidly in a back
and forth motion
particular to their species.
Monica said it means
they want to be fed.
Their parents are likely
deeper in the stand
of trees being careful.
The wind has a metal hand.
Around them the city
explodes with helicopters
and tourists but here
on Francisco Street where
you also live this yard
is protected but not quiet.
I can hear the Russian
woman talking out
the window, I catch
a few words, one
of which sounds like
"object force." It makes
me think of Anna
who is probably married
to that Finnish Brazilian

martial arts instructor.
That was afternoon.
Now it is later,
much, the absolute
worst pure center
of night, for an hour
in bed I resisted coming
here to my desk
to search for those terrible
destructive questions still
hiding from me.
Do you do that? Or
is there some other way?
I thought I might
but I can't see
the yard at all, just
some yellow safety
lights in the alley. I try
to keep the chair
from creaking, I know
Sarah knows in her sleep
I am in my study,
disturbed. I wish
I could send the word
asylum out very far
into the air like a clear
colorless substance
all my friends could
breathe in sleep, you
can never protect
everyone. That constant
humming sound is time
coming to take us
away from each other.
Or the refrigerator,

keeping the milk cold
and pure. So much
noise all the time
in the city, do you like it?
You must, you stay.
Last week I limped
in my giant ridiculous cast
one block to get coffee
on the corner and sat
outside feeling very sorry
but also happy. You
sat next to me and I was
pretty sure you
were you but I didn't
know. I gave you
my *New York Times*
and we talked about torture
and baseball and how
many more weeks
are left for newspapers.
And then you asked me
if I'd ever be able to walk again.
That's what it's like
to be eighty I thought
but I don't know. Nothing's
natural to me anymore.
I forgot to buy a light bulb.
Now in the afternoon
the blades of grass
are completely still. No one
tends a little television
in the Russian woman's window.
All I know is I have tried
for a long time to be useful,
like everyone I am also

always balancing
on the small blade of not
letting other people down.
Now it is getting darker.
Orange nasturtiums
you can go out and gather
and place directly into a salad
are glowing, and pink
roses wander along
the very old green wooden
trellis towards the blue shed
where Ephraim carefully traces
his engineering plans
for great structures
that will never be built
at least in the few
decades of his lifetime
remaining. He walks
with a little hunch towards
me to collect my rent
check and I am holding it
out to him both of us
with matching apologetic smiles.
In Oklahoma once
I ate blueberries, I
recall they tasted like lake.
If dust is particles
of our skin why
is there more each
time I return?
I know tomorrow
I will sit in that dark
before daylight without
a name, and feeling
the last few drops

of water from the shower
still on her shoulders
she will come and stand
next to me where I am
at my desk pushing
against one word feeling
its hinge creak like wind
would a gate if it could feel
anything at all.

III

Journey Through the Past

Listening to Neil Young in California
is like throwing away the old pills

that used to cure something and turning
your face towards the day, i.e. the ocean

filling the window with grey boats
floating in totally bright present aloneness.

For several weeks on my laptop
I had a picture of the space shuttle docking.

Then I replaced it with the ravenous
woolly adelgid covering a blighted eastern hemlock.

One branch looks like a limb
destroyed by an improvised explosive device.

Friend whose father is dying,
let us exchange dreams.

I am strong enough for yours
and you can move

down the long boring beige literal corridor
and replace the batteries in the thermostat,

fingering a diamond hair clip.

Travelers Among Mountains and Streams

Today I have the feeling no matter
which way I turn my head I am
into ideas like everyone is freer than me
painlessly bonking whatever
is the mental equivalent of my nose.
My actual one itches, it's the plum
trees shedding invisible sexual particles.
Onto the streets I go and see the horrible
charming Victorians of my new home
San Francisco where I have moved for love.
Like purple plastic wedding dresses
they are ready to be left out imperviously
in the rain. Let's put down the book
about the later phase of Le Corbusier
when he planned the perfect harmonic
Indian city of Chandigarh and pick up
one about makers of an early type
of Japanese kimono called the kosode.
On them sometimes artists painted
landscapes such as *Kosode with Tree
and Flowering Plants* by Sakai Hōitsu.
Like the little figures in the picture
through the picture we journey slowly
with our eyes closely observing mountain
formations, a waterfall, trees, a village,
and tiny figures of travelers just like us.
Once the silk over someone's body
rippled, now the kimono hangs
on a wall. Oh lifestyle! Oh cake!
Between my ears is drifting now
the strange translucent golden word
axolotl. Through its whole life it never

grows any older. Through its shoulders
you can see its blood. Thousands of miles
away THE EAST a kingdom covered
by giant clouds. Where was I born? Among
human faces, deep in the sun of a real
young mother, under blowing unmagical snow.

Poem for San Francisco

Afternoon, almost
too bright to stare at directly,
also contains dark shapes. Black windows
in the old converted warehouses
filled now with new industry.
Shadows cast by telephone poles. So many
wires everywhere, how is it
I have never truly seen
all the infrastructure and methods
over my head everywhere
in this city I go? I think
they are quite beautiful. Always
the wires are unexpectedly framing
parts of the sky and all
natural and human things it contains,
making transitory paintings the very
subject of which is cloud motion. Truly
I fear animals. Now I am growing
very analytical. A kind of
peacefulness into me carefully
moves like a grasshopper
into a room full of totally believable metal
grass and trees. There is one great bridge
at the edge of the city falling asleep. And another
humming an orange welcoming song.

Kingdom Come

She asked me how long it will be
until the giant black rose
she has seen in her dreams
bursts out of the ocean just beyond
the walls of the circular city
and drips molten fire on the heads
of likenesses of the smiling gods
who sent a message from outside
our solar system crying
and swearing to protect us
if we built them. Quite
a long time. Probably many
hundreds of years. First we must
build the circular walls,
then the towers and the steps.
Then we must build the satellite array
and send it into the atmosphere.
And we don't have that
technology yet. The scientists
who can dream of building it
have not yet even been born. So
for now I say to her let us live
here in this apartment and make
sounds of love on this futon
while outside the window the orange
extension cable strangles
the white and green flowering branch
and monks cry anciently on the radio.

Letter to a Lover

Today I am going to pick you up at the beige airport.
My heart feels like a field of calves in the sun.
My heart is wired directly to the power source of mediocre songs.
I am trying to catch a ray of sunlight in my mouth.

I look forward to showing you my new furniture.
I look forward to the telephone ringing, it is not you,
you are in the kitchen trying to figure out the coffeemaker,
you are pouring out the contents of your backpack.

I wonder if you now have golden fur?
I wonder if your arsenal of kind remarks is empty?
I remember when I met you you were wearing a grey dress,
that was also blue, not unlike the water plus the sky.

They say it's difficult to put a leash on a hummingbird.
So let us be no longer the actuary of each other!
Let us bow no longer our heads to the tyranny of numbers!
Hurry off the plane, with your rhinestone covered bag

full of magazines that check up on the downfall of the stars.
I will be waiting for you at the bottom of the moving stairs.

Frankenstein Love

I think there was a movie once
where Frankenstein fell in love with a vampire.
A small mummy at first interfered
but later provided the requisite necessary
clarifications. He can only
meet you at night. Her face
is scarred in a permanent expression
of doom, but her bolt glows whenever
she sees you. The rival for the vampire's affections
was a vaguely feminine zombie. Frankenstein
felt not very mysterious. Many different
feelings cycled below whoever's
skin she had been given. Did they even
belong to her? In the many pages
of the book of love this is only one story.
But everyone goes through it once. The main
question is, will you be the one unable
to control your temper, sewed together
as you are from the past? Or the one
who always ends up turning away in search
of another likeness?

White Castle

In Wichita Kansas my friends ordered square burgers
with mysterious holes leaking a delicious substance
that would fuel us in all sorts of necessary beautiful ways
for our long journey eastward versus the night.
I was outside touching my hand to the rough
surface of the original White Castle. I was thinking
major feelings such as longing for purpose
plunge down one like the knowledge one
has been drinking water for one's whole life
and never actually seen a well, and minor ones
we never name are always across the surface
of every face every three seconds or so rippling
and producing in turn other feelings. Oh regarder,
if I call this one green bee mating with a dragonfly
in pain it will already be too late for both of us.
I am here with that one gone and now inside this one
I am right now naming feeling of having named
something already gone, and you just about to know
I saw gentle insects crawling in a line from a crack
in the corner of the base of the original White Castle
towards only they know what point in the darkness.

Screaming Skull

Near Geneva the Hadron Collider
lies underground. Almost
complete, whispers the giant
screaming skull. Your species
is obsessed with the search
for tiny links in the chain you do
not know leads to the collar
of an enormous dragon. You
have fallen completely in love
with metal thinking. You are in great
immaculate aluminum vats
that make the tiny workers
in their suits and helmets glint
a ferocious silver cooling
sections of the giant collider
and preparing to send pulses
of proton beams through it
in opposing directions. Detectors
will sort the microscopic
particles searching for the elusive
Higgs boson or strangelets.
For years beneath the sea I have
been dreaming of the proper time
to emerge and signal my ally the Sun
to rain fire down on all
your towers. Together we
with our retarded cousin the Moon
would watch your cities sink
into the boiling oceans. You search
for the grand unified theory
but will find only a tiny black hole
we will all be sucked into.
And now I will never have my revenge!

Ceasing to Be

The idea is simple. Lucretius wanted to rid
the world of death fear by writing
On the Nature of Things. He says we fear
death only believing the mind somehow
continues even after the skull that holds it
is broken and harmless vapor leaks out
into everything dissolving. It's
true I fear my death, but I fear
the death of others more, because that's
a death without death through which
I must live. Or I fear my death
for the death others will have to live through
without me. That and probably pain
are why people are afraid. Anyway a world
without death fear would be even more scary.
Not that it matters. Death and fear. One
hand of steel, one of gold. Even you
wouldn't know which to cut off or reach
out for first, Lucretius, because it is always
very dark here in the future.

Sad News

We have some sad news this morning
from Mars. But I'm thinking about lions. Someone
said something salient and my head became
a light bulb full of power exactly

the shape of my head. Sinister thoughts
at the Xerox machine. A chat with a retired
torturer. Now the sharp blade. Apparently
some solar wind pushed a few specklets of actually

not red but grey Mars dust through the seal
into the vacuum where the very tiny oiled hydraulics
of the light from the distant future collector seized.
What was it my brother said to me once? Like

a vampire bat on a unicorn Change rides
every moment. Houston is full of dead elephants
and empty labs experimenting on silence, open any mouth
and out blows some hope in a binary data stream.

Poem for Jim Zorn

in the photograph you are holding a green helmet
and smiling directly into the future

but *the straight and the square rarely advance*

a Chinese poet working a minor bureaucratic post
a few miles north of the capital
wrote 1200 years ago

when they called the emperor The Immortal

I know you tried
but a falseness runs through all our dealings

a seahawk is not even a real bird

and somewhere it is still 1976
and I have just lofted
a football over the head of my very cold brother

who turns in his blue down coat
that used to belong to me

and runs with his arms stretched
out as far as he can

towards the pine trees
and I fear when he comes back

he will tell me something everyone knows

The Pavilion of Vague Blues

In the airport bar the lady singer's
voice reminded him of a blue
praying mantis he had seen
in a painting riding on
the shoulder of a very young
knight into battle. She was
singing about how she felt
always full of emptiness. He could
almost physically grasp what
that meant. Then he did.
Then he knew he would never
be happier than when he was
living in that medium-sized
Midwestern city, writing stories
about the lives of the inhabitants
of its highest skyscraper.
He could see exactly what
it looked like then, shining upward
like an ancient lighthouse
in the snow. He saw a man
with a beer reading a book
called *8 Amazing Things You Do
Not Know.* Now she was
looking at him, singing about flying
in wondering circles above your life.
On the placard it said she was
available for all events except funerals.
Her name was Lady McDust.

Fortune

I went last night to see a Chinese movie
with an old friend who seems to love
everything. Equanimity I can only
aspire towards like a leaf or a reflection
of a tower in a pond. The entire
movie took place inside a storm
of totally synthesized feelings. A father
and son leave the city on a desultory
journey out into the countryside
for the mystical purpose of dropping
a stone into a well. Periodically they are
assaulted for a time then joined
by monks who guard citadels presumably
filled with riches or ancient instructive texts.
Every time just as I started to like
a character he would be assassinated
right before my eyes by ninjas or meet
some other horrible unjustified fate.
One particularly mild Shaolin monk leaned
against a wall and his shoulder fell off
and his hair attacked his face. Fortune
said the subtitles is a giant dragon
with flowers in its antlers. A widow
in a white dress appeared in the father's
dream then emerged into the actual
world and caressed the face of the child.
They walked off towards the well. The stone
glowed in a close-up. Decades passed.
Then the music suddenly stopped
and I found myself holding an empty
bag of popcorn I don't remember eating.
Goodbye I said to my friend but she

had already long ago gone off into the future
to feed her brand new digital snake
a couple of digital crickets.

Charmer

That man looks like a snake charmer
Rufus said, holding his beer. That
man has skills. Rufus works
with me at the university. Border
wars, rebellions, inspectors. Like
a 9th century T'ang Dynasty bureaucrat
Rufus had survived them all. He
told me about several attempts
on his life disguised as practical jokes
and birthday parties. The department
secretary it's true does bare
her teeth when you come near
the Xerox machine like a beaver fearing
an enema. Years ago Rufus read
a book about Zeno of Citium and invented
a brilliant infallible system of relying
on divine intelligence to organize
university forms. No longer
did he try to shape circumstances
to his desires. The world is a blindly
running machine. Now he is ever
more slowly coasting towards
without reaching total stasis. His desk
is a medium sized wooden lake
on which float two staplers. I don't
even remember where I was born.
I might be a replicant. How would
I know? The snake charmer was sitting
at the bar, holding a glass full
of ice and clear liquid, watching a game.
I had to admit he had the air
of someone wearing a turban.
Any skills he had were very well hidden.

This Little Game

When I'm washing my hands I think of a name
of someone I don't know. Like Evangeline
or Rufus or BobBob. And I sing Happy Birthday
inserting that name at the proper time,
stopping only and turning off the water
when I reach the end of the song. This
little game ensures I am washing my hands
just long enough for the little soap particles
to bind to all the nasty dirt ones
and wash them down the drain.
Which makes me feel protected.
Like going to what we called "temple"
but actually was a church we shared
with some Ursulines, an order of Christians
dedicated to the education of girls and care
of the sick and otherwise needy. We
used it on Friday nights and Saturday days
and they on Sundays of course, sometimes
Saturday evenings all full of emptiness
troubles and peace and done with our final
service we saw them crossing the street
and moving like phantoms towards the building
already no longer ours. In the lobby
there was a giant baptismal font made of stone
and at Christmas little carvings of Jesus
on the cross hung up on every wall. None
of us cared and we thought ourselves
good and brave for sharing and also safe
from all true Christian soldiers. Never
with terrible swords made of virtue and light
shall they trouble us, they shall pass us by.

To a Predator

I woke up early and saw a fox.
It was leaping and dragging its glorious
red and white tail behind it across
the road. It held a grasshopper in its mouth,
which it dropped when it saw the small
carcass of a young javelina. Last night
I was woken by their hairless rooting through
a field of cactus in moonlight. They all
stood together, ears rotated forward into
the breeze, protecting the single mother
protecting a pair of young. Their
mustachioed labium superius oris i.e.
upper lip protects a gentle tusk
the color of greywater. I almost sympathize
with their corporate need to snuffle
and roam in packs until dawn returns them
to hollows they made in the ground.
But my sleep does not. Thus I shone
a very powerful flashlight into their midst
and watched them scramble across
the highway, dispersing. Thus I walked
out into this morning, wearing a shirt
the color of a dandelion, whistling
an uncertain tune about the mild unequal
life I would like to know better of a rich
acquaintance in the Mexican city of Guadalajara.

Global Warming

In old black and white documentaries
sometimes you can see
the young at a concert or demonstration
staring in a certain way as if
a giant golden banjo
is somewhere sparkling
just too far off to hear.
They really didn't know there was a camera.
Cross legged on the lawn
they are patiently listening to speeches
or the folk singer hunched
over his little brown guitar.
They look as tired as the young today.
The calm manner in which their eyes
just like the camera rest
on certain things then move
to others shows they know
no amount of sunlight
will keep them from growing suddenly older.
I have seen the new five-dollar bills
with their huge pink hypertrophied numbers
in the lower right hand corner and feel
excited and betrayed.
Which things should never change?
The famous cherry trees
I grew up under
drop all their brand new buds
a little earlier each year.
Now it's all over before the festival begins.
The young.
Maybe they'll let us be in their dreams.

A Summer Rainstorm

Sometimes I am happy to be
here in this bright room

drifting through music made by others

looking down on the heads of the people passing
teaching each other that life is forgoing

I think everyone I can see is partially sad
because we will never be fully forgiven

this apartment building has seen so much moving through the city

well ordered troops
many proud careful mothers and fathers pushing carriages

many people holding hands or talking on their cell phones and crying
hundreds of girls each wearing a plastic tiara

carefully placed on her head by the mayor at the annual spring parade

this building with the ordinary green facade
no one will see as they wait for the storm to pass

their breath creating giant cloud forms

from my window I can see their heads

it makes me smile a little with love how much they look like moose in
        the zoo
how they stand very patiently close to one another

under the door of the sky
their memories gracefully blundering into the long cool forest

full of shadows

our life is the one we already have

The Painted Desert

Right now in the rest area it's sunny and cold. Someone
is taking a picture of the vending machine. I have
never been sad for appropriate reasons. Never
have I sat in the wet grass looking not at dark sky
but blue paper someone had carefully taken
hours to punch out in a shape invisible
until the flashlight is turned on below. Earlier
when I said everything is a switch immediately
the interlocking gears in the self-hatred mechanism
began to grind. Part of me is always about to turn
in a direction I will never go. Trucks roar
filled with things people need. Sometimes I sound
to myself like a robot. Too many times as a teen
I stared onto the surface of a mysterious
solvable multifaceted cube. I can see you don't need
me to stretch out my hand to point to dread
and its little button. The door swings open,
one entire miserable summer I should have been happy
flashes in the word molybdenum. I saw people
mining cinder from volcanoes. Cinder
is made into blocks lighter than cement to hold
the plywood shelves holding one or more
than one person's books. To intermingle
is so difficult to extricate. Shells marine organisms
abandon dissolve into ooze. Found near waterfalls
it's known as travertine. Goodbye, someday
I'll invent the magic lantern, then music,
then whatever's the opposite of the need
to control everything so it can be perfect for you.

For You in Full Bloom

In the park the giant gold head
of some expired tyrant

watches everyone
breathing and thinking

old mothers with their prams
solitary lovers
not realizing they are stretching

out their fingers and grasping the air

during the day the gold dome
of his head
grows unbearably hot

then during the night
cools when no one is in the garden
but the trees

with their leaves like words in a dictionary
you can imagine touching
but never quite reach

and feel a little power and wonder
who is truly happy

the tyrant was a very geometric planner

so he built these boulevards
and homes with their metal mansard roofs
that tilt a little backward

making attics
people like to live in
even though the rain

is loud as it falls easily off of the metal roofs into the street

outside the window I see green leaves moving
closer to each other in the breeze
over a comically diminutive black electric car

a woman wearing a blue cloak
touches a device in her hair

this morning you left
by means of the futuristic light-rail system

today my mouth
is an artificial lake
I am too tired to swim across

later I will read

but for now I must sit very still
and think of the city
as a body that changes

and probably will not live forever

or an instrument that plays a giant song
no one will ever be large enough to hear

roads lead to the peripheries
dizzyingly through the two chief lungs

which are two great forests
full of trees filtering the air
my particular lime green railing
tings

again the song begins

This Handwriting

This afternoon I heard
the small voice speaking again,
though no one was there.
I could not hear the words
though from the helpless
complicated tone I knew
it was something like
someday you will realize
you already know you must go
elsewhere to be free.
Maybe the white island
with just a few necessary buildings
you saw once from above
as if you were flying.
All your friends in gentle
laughing disputation are already
waiting. For now I settle
for trying to picture
each of their faces.
But when I close my eyes
I just keep seeing this horrible
actual sunny floor I have
scattered pages of my handwriting
on, searching for a pattern.
And also this table. Upon
it lies a yellow book containing
a translation of the half-burned
gospel that says often Jesus
kissed Mary on the mouth.
Reading it makes me feel
as if the true future like the son
of a dethroned king long ago

hid in a cave, trying to silence
its breathing. The great
black indeterminate stallion
pounded implacably by.
Now there is only silence
like an auditorium after
a modern composition
had just finished perfectly
destroying our foolish
cherished ideas of music.
When I think very hard
about my thoughts they seem
to me to be very small horses
attached to invisible reins
attached to facts. And what
of my memories? Like sleeping
in daylight. A decade ago
I lived in Massachusetts,
a shallow terrible installation
leaking smoky versions
of myself, each in turn
emitting weak soluble ideas
like people care only because
they do not even know
they feel they must. And now
I am here in California,
happy to be though always
part of me is thinking of my friends
and their shadows, patiently
waiting for my shadow to join them.

IV

Come On All You Ghosts

1

I heard a little cough
in the room, and turned
but no one was there

except the flowers
Sarah bought me
and my death's head

glow in the dark key chain
that lights up and moans
when I press the button

on top of its skull
and the ghost
I shyly name Aglow.

Are you there Aglow
I said in my mind
reader, exactly the way

you just heard it
in yours about four
poem time units ago

unless you have already
put down the paper directly
after the mention

of poetry or ghosts.
Readers I am sorry
for some of you

this is not a novel.
Goodbye. Now it is just
us and the death's head

and the flowers and the ghost
in San Francisco thinking
together by means

of the ancient transmission device.
I am sorry
but together we are

right now thinking
along by means
of an ancient mechanistic

system no one invented
involving super-microscopic
particles that somehow

(weird!) enter through
your eyes or ears
depending on where

you are right now
reading or listening.
To me it seems

like being together
one body made of light
clanging down through

a metal structure
for pleasure and edification.
Reader when I think of you

you are in a giant purple chair
in a Starbucks gradually leaking power
while Neil Young

eats a campfire then drinks
a glass of tears
on satellite radio.

Hello. I am 40.
I have lived in Maryland,
Amherst, San Francisco,

New York, Ljubljana,
Stonington (house
of the great ornate wooden frame

holding the mirror the dead
saw us in whenever
we walked past)

New Hampshire at the base
of the White Mountains
on clear blue days

full of dark blue jays
beyond emotion jaggedly piercing,
Minneapolis of which

I have spoken
earlier and quite enough,
Paris and now

San Francisco again.
Reader, you are right now
in what for me is the future

experiencing something
you cannot
without this poem.

I myself am suspicious
and cruel. Sometimes
when I close my eyes

I hear a billion workers
in my skull
hammering nails from which

all the things I see
get hung. But poems
are not museums,

they are machines
made of words,
you pour as best

you can your attention
in and in you the poetic
state of mind is produced

said one of the many
French poets with whom
I feel I must agree.

Another I know
writes his poems on silver
paint in a mirror.

I feel like a president
raising his fist in the sun.

2

Reader, it doesn't seem
very strange to be
here in this apartment

thinking of you
and how we will someday
(right now!) be together.

I hear hammering,
workmen are fixing
the front steps,

as I step out over them
into the morning
my mind is wearing

a black suit
like a funeral director's assistant
prepared for very serious work

that has nothing to do with me.
Now in the café
very carefully blasting

my veins with coffee
asking what do we know
and what can we learn?

above me a painted waterfall
and stars on the ceiling
all this peace

makes me feel queer
the mysteries
the mysteries

we could never have predicted
they become our lives
and less confused

calmly in them
we rotate not psychotic or tragic.
I have lived in the black crater

of feeling every moment
is the moment just after
one has chosen forever

to live in the black crater
of having chosen to live in the black crater
and therefore I know

exactly why David Foster Wallace
took his life away from himself
even though he was also taking it away

from everyone he knew.
This morning I was woken
by soft sour breath

a slight fleck of metal
in the organic
like a field of titanium gravestones

growing warmer in the sun.
I could breathe it for hours
but now it is gone

which is ok as long as long as the exhaling
somewhere else continues.
Her job is to incrementally

regulate the conduct
of those who regulate
the city and mine is to be

happy for a few moments thinking
I could actually be
one who is happy watching

afternoon fog pour
predictably down
into sunny Noe Valley

from cold Twin Peaks.

3

If you know
the story of Marco Polo
you know after a long journey he came

upon the Mongol armies sleeping
and wisely turned back
already composing

a much more fabulous story
than not being able
to report being torn

apart by four horses
attached to his limbs.
From then on wherever

he went or did not he brought back
wondrous marvels and lies.
In this poem

every word means exactly
what it means
when we use it in every day life.

So when I say I went
to the grocery store
and felt too ashamed

to ask where are the eggs
only a very small part of me means
I have returned to report

we have by our mothers
been permanently destroyed.
When the president

opens his hands
a door knob
made of an unnaturally

heavy substance
floats up to the blue
door to the worry factory.

Open it and down
drift all the 21st century
problems, stick out

your tongue and maybe
you will taste sunlight
and maybe ash.

Go little president!
We are all blowing
into your wings!

We promise to no longer
be transactional
in our personal dealings!

We promise no longer
to know some things
are important but one

does not need to know why.
If the heart makes
the sound of two violins

sleeping in a baby carriage,
then new technologies
cannot make us

both more loyal and free.
Wayward free radical dreams,
I want to be loyal,

I say it once into the darkness.
Come on all you ghosts,
try to make me forget you.

4

Come with me
and I will show you
terrible marvels.

The little cough I heard in my mind
was one I remembered
my father made just as he died,

we weren't sure
if it was his last breath
or just some air left in his lungs,

not that it matters.
Please don't feel the least bit sorry
for me or yourself,

everyone you have ever seen
has a dead father,
some are just walking around alive

but it's temporary,
so bring your sorrow
for everyone out into the street,

in the sun. If a nation
can fall asleep
it can wake up not

exactly angry but a little dizzy
with pleasant hunger.
A glass of juice.

A melancholy. Then remember
we all have something important
to do today in the sun.

Come on all you ghosts,
all you young holding hands
or alone, all you older

people and people of middle
indeterminate age,
we need you, winter is not

through with us.
The sea seems more
than a little angry,

and over it blows
a very cold breeze
that is also the color grey.

In this room with its black desk
sometimes I hear
the crystal factory whirring

under a sky
the color of black
tabletops entranceways

and dead light bulbs.
Are those your hands
on the switches

ghosts? All day I have been
feeling blind, dizzy and enclosed,
as if I were being carried

in the hand of a great being
who insisted he was still
but I could feel the motion.

5

Come on all you ghosts.
Bring me your lucky numbers
that failed you, bring me

your boots made of the skin
of placid animals
who stood for a while in the snow.

Bring me your books
made of blue sky
stitched together with thread

made of the memory
of how warm
even the most terrible

among us has felt
the skin of his or her beloved
in the morning to be.

Come on all you ghosts,
try to make me forget
one summer lost

in a reservoir and another
I keep in my chest.
Come on all you ghosts,

try to make me repeat
the most terrible thing I said
to someone and I will

if the mind of that someone
could ever be eased.
Come on let's vote

for no one in the election
of who is next to die.
Come on all you ghosts,

I know you can hear me,
I know you are here,
I have heard you cough

and sigh when I pretend
I do not believe
I have to say something important.

Probably no one will die
of anything I say.
Probably no one will live

even a second longer.
Is that true?
Come on all you ghosts,

you can tell me now,
I have seen one of you becoming
and I am no longer afraid,

just sad for everyone
but also happy this morning I woke
next to the warm skin

of my beloved. I do not know
what terrible marvels
tomorrow will bring

but ghosts if I must join you
you and I know
I have done my best to leave

behind this machine
anyone with a mind
who cares can enter.

About the Author

Matthew Zapruder is the author of two previous collections of poetry, *American Linden* (Tupelo Press, 2002) and *The Pajamaist* (Copper Canyon Press, 2006). *The Pajamaist* was selected by Tony Hoagland as the winner of the William Carlos Williams Award from the Poetry Society of America, and was chosen by *Library Journal* as one of the top ten poetry volumes of 2006. He is also co-translator from Romanian, with historian Radu Ioanid, of *Secret Weapon: Selected Late Poems of Eugen Jebeleanu* (Coffee House Press, 2008). German- and Slovene-language editions of his poems have been published by Luxbooks and Šerpa Editions; in 2009, Luxbooks also published a separate German-language graphic-novel version of the poem "The Pajamaist." A collaborative book with painter Chris Uphues, *For You in Full Bloom*, was published by Pilot Books in 2009. His work has appeared in many anthologies, including *Third Rail: The Poetry of Rock and Roll; Legitimate Dangers: American Poets of the New Century; Seriously Funny: Poems about Love, Death, Religion, Art, Politics, Sex, and Everything;* and *The Best American Poetry 2009.* He has been a Lannan Literary Fellow in Marfa, Texas, and a recipient of a May Sarton prize from the American Academy of Arts and Sciences. He lives in San Francisco.

The Chinese character for poetry is made up of two parts: "word" and "temple." It also serves as pressmark for Copper Canyon Press.

Since 1972, Copper Canyon Press has fostered the work of emerging, established, and world-renowned poets for an expanding audience. The Press thrives with the generous patronage of readers, writers, booksellers, librarians, teachers, students, and funders—everyone who shares the belief that poetry is vital to language and living.

Major funding has been provided by:
Amazon.com
Anonymous
Beroz Ferrell & The Point, LLC
Golden Lasso, LLC
Lannan Foundation
National Endowment for the Arts
Cynthia Lovelace Sears and Frank Buxton
William and Ruth True
Washington State Arts Commission
Charles and Barbara Wright

For information and catalogs:
COPPER CANYON PRESS
Post Office Box 271
Port Townsend, Washington 98368
360-385-4925
www.coppercanyonpress.org

Copper Canyon Press gratefully acknowledges board member Jim Wickwire in honor of his many years of service to poetry and independent publishing.

The poems have been typeset in Sabon, an old-style serif typeface designed by the German-born typographer and designer Jan Tschichold (1902–1974) in the period 1964–1967. Headings are set in Gotham, a sans serif typeface by Hoefler & Frere-Jones. Book design and composition by Phil Kovacevich. Printed on archival-quality paper at McNaughton & Gunn, Inc.